❧ Nando's ❧

INDOOR

RECIPES FOR EVERYONE

At last! The collection of
Nando's recipes you've been
asking us for......

Peri-delicious and peri-simple
to make, there's one for every
occasion.

All our favourite indoor recipes
are at the front of the book,
simply turn the book over to
find our wonderful outdoor
recipes.

Enjoy!

Nando's is not just about chicken, it's never just been about chicken

It's about pride, passion, courage, integrity and most of all, family

Today Nando's has over 400 restaurants world-wide in over 30 countries, spreading from Angola to Zimbabwe, the UK to Australia and many places in between. Each restaurant is unique, a part of it's own local community, but in each restaurant you will experience the same feeling of warmth and family, the same relaxed atmosphere.

In our restaurants we encourage noise, we encourage people to use their hands when eating and we encourage family gatherings in the spirit of the good old days. Our motto is that children should be seen and heard. All we ask is that people smile and enjoy themselves.

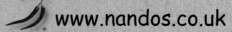

www.nandos.co.uk

Let us entertain you
page 50-69

Igniting the flame

Two friends, an exceptional recipe for Peri-Peri, flame grilled chicken and a dream. It was in the small suburb of Rosettenville, Johannesburg, in a humble eatery called Chickenland that a dream was destined to become a reality in a few short years. There, in the heart of the local Portuguese community, chicken was prepared and enjoyed according to a centuries old Portuguese tradition – the delicious and well kept secret of the tightly knit community.

The friends had no idea that they were igniting the Nando's flame; a flame that would first be carried throughout South Africa and then spread globally.

Bottling the fire!

As the restaurants spread around the world, it was not long before Nando's decided to bottle the 'Nando's experience' with a range of Peri-Peri Sauces to inspire adventurous cooking at home.

Marinades and a Cooking Sauce range were soon to follow, bringing a world of full flavour, exotic tastes, quality and convenience to the supermarket shelves.

The Legend behind our Logo!

The story of the Barcelos Cockerel may date back to the 14th century, but the sentiments expressed in this ancient tale are still relevant today. A pilgrim passing through Barcelos, a small town in Portugal, was accused of theft - an accusation that he strongly denied, and no wonder as the penalty for this crime was death. Alone and in a strange village, he had only his faith to help him. So, he appealed to Our Lady, and St James, the Patron Saint of Protection, for justice to be done.

He was brought before the Judge, who already had quite a lot on his plate in the most literal sense. You see, he was about to start eating his dinner of a whole roast cockerel. The pilgrim pleaded his innocence and requested divine intervention, saying "If I am innocent, may that cockerel get up and crow!"

The cockerel immediately got up and started to crow loudly. Whether the cockerel lay down again to be eaten by the Judge is anyone's guess, but from that day forward the cockerel symbol became synonymous with faith, justice and good luck.

 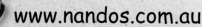

Key: some handy symbols you will need as you try out our delicious recipes.

Marinate over night

Suitable for vegetarians

15
Preparation time in minutes

20
Cooking time in minutes

The source of the sauce

It was in Africa, with its rich soils, majestic thunderstorms and intense heat, that the explorers discovered a small treasure, the African Birds Eye Chilli. This fiery little chilli, known to the locals as Peri-Peri, soon became an essential ingredient in their cuisine. Although explosively hot, Peri-Peri allows for a unique and delicious flavour when used in moderation.

Nando's Peri-Peri Sauce is a blend of sun-ripened lemons, a dash of garlic, herbs, spices and the African Birds Eye Chilli. The recipe for Nando's famous Peri-Peri blend is a closely guarded family secret that has been handed down through the generations. Nando's Peri-Peri is the essence of the restaurants and the bottled sauces; a delicious combination of flavour and heat. Peri-Peri also has proven nutritional benefits, being rich in vitamins A and C, it acts as an effective decongestant, thins the blood and can aid digestion. It is also known to contain aphrodisiac properties. In fact, so strong are the legends of the aphrodisiac powers of Peri-Peri that, in early times, it was prohibited for consumption both within ancient monasteries and, more recently, in prisons.

The higher the rating the hotter the chilli

Number of servings

Names: some ingredients have different names in different countries. Here's a couple we have highlighted.

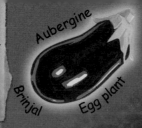

Aubergine / Brinjal / Egg plant

Capsicum / Pepper

The science of chillies

Chilli plants belong to the genus Capsicum of which there are more than two hundred known varieties. This family is characterised by the presence of capsicum (the chemical substance that causes the chilli to taste hot) on the veins inside the chilli and not in the seeds as is generally believed. Not all chillies contain the same amount of capsicum and therefore cause different oral sensations ranging from a mild tingling sensation to an intense heat when eaten.

Contrary to popular belief chilli is not just about heat. Each variety also boasts a unique flavour, such as the mild tropical flavour of the Habanero chilli or the heavy, smoky, tobacco flavour of the Ancho chilli.

In 1912 a pharmacist called Wilbur Scoville devised a scientific method to measure the amount of capsicum in a chilli. He named this method "Scoville Heat Units" - a scale ranging from 10 to 1,000,000 - indicating the amount of water required to neutralise the heat.

Chill out!

To cool down when eating chillies try drinking milk or eating ice cream or yoghurt. Because capsicum is soluble in oil not water, it dissolves in the fat globules of dairy products and will be washed away when swallowed. Don't think of beer or fizzy drinks – the carbon dioxide has an irritant effect on the open nerve endings and will increase the burning sensation.

Cups

A cup is 250ml, or measure out using a cup rather than a mug

Our Peri-ometer

On each of the Nando's sauces you'll find our Peri-ometer, which shows how hot we think the sauce is – though not everyone agrees with us! If you find any of our sauces too hot we recommend adding some crème fraiche, and if you think our sauces aren't hot enough then you can add some of our Hot Peri-Peri Sauce to liven it up!

PERIOMETER
EXTRA HOT
HOT
Medium
Mild
Heat Indicator

Pepper
10 to 100

Jalapeno
2,500 to 5,000

Peri-Peri
12,000 to 20,000

Habanero
200,000 to 300,000

Love at first bite

Hazel's favourite recipe is the Nando's Peri-Peri Chicken Caesar Salad; quick to make, tasty and healthy. Hazel has worked for Nando's for 10 years, originally in South Africa. More recently she took on the job of introducing Nando's Peri-Peri Sauces to Australia.

Peri-Peri Chicken Caesar Salad

Ingredients

Salad

1 jar	**Nando's Hot Peri-Peri Marinade**
4	**chicken breasts each sliced into 3 chunky strips**
2	**cos lettuces shred into 1/2 " slices**
1 tbsp	**grated parmesan**
	parmesan shavings to garnish
	ground black pepper to garnish

Sauce

4 tbsp	**mayonnaise**
1 tsp	**anchovy paste**
2 tsp	**Worcestershire Sauce**
1/2 tsp	**black pepper**
1 tbsp	**fresh lemon juice**
1 tbsp	**grated parmesan**

Croutons

1/2	**part-baked Ciabatta loaf**
3 tbsp	**olive oil**
	sea salt

Method:

- Put the marinade in a large bowl and add the chicken strips. Set aside.
- Dice the bread into 1" cubes.
- Heat the oil in a wide sauté pan and fry the bread for 2-3 minutes until golden all over.
- Drain on paper towels, sprinkle with salt and allow to cool.
- In a bowl, thoroughly mix together all the ingredients for the sauce and set aside.
- Cook the chicken either in a sauté pan, under the grill or on the BBQ.
- Put the shredded lettuce into a large bowl.
- Pour over the Caesar sauce and 1/2 of the croutons.
- Mix thoroughly and divide between large 4 plates or pasta bowls.
- Top with the hot chicken strips, the remaining croutons, parmesan and black pepper.

Peri-Peri Salmon Linguine

Method:

- Use a good, heavy based, large frying pan.
- Add enough olive oil, plus the butter, to be able to coat the base of the pan.
- Stir-fry the garlic till golden.
- When sizzling add the salmon, skin side down, and cook for 3-5 mins over a high heat to crisp the skin.
- Then, add the balance of the olive oil and all the Peri-Peri (careful – it will sizzle at this stage), turn the salmon and cook for a further few minutes until cooked through.
- Remove the salmon from the pan and set aside.
- Place the cooked linguine, together with the rocket, into the pan in which the salmon was cooked and toss the remaining pan oils through.
- Serve the linguine in oversized pasta plates, with a piece of salmon on top of each portion.
- Sprinkle with salt, cracked black pepper and parmesan shavings.

Ingredients

½ cup	extra virgin olive oil (approx)
1 tbsp	butter
3-4	cloves fresh garlic, crushed
1kg	fresh salmon, cut into 4 generous pieces
80ml	Nando's Medium Peri-Peri Sauce
200g	fresh baby rocket
1 pkt	linguine (fresh if possible), cooked

Pan-fried Fish with Peri-Peri

Method:

- Marinate the fish fillets in the Peri-Peri for at least a couple of hours.

- Mix the yoghurt with the Lime & Coriander Marinade and set aside.

- Dust the fillets in the flour and tap off any excess.

- Heat a little olive oil and butter in a sauté pan and gently fry the fish until cooked - about 4 mins each side.

- Remove the fish and set aside.

- Tip out any remaining oil and butter, put the pan back on the heat and deglaze with a teaspoon of Peri-Peri Sauce.

- Place the fillets on top of the salad leaves, drizzle over the pan juices and the lime & coriander yoghurt and garnish with lime wedges and sprigs of coriander.

Ingredients

2	firm white fish fillets (e.g. cod)
1 jar	Nando's Peri-Peri Sauce (choose your favourite)
	seasoned flour for dusting
	oil and butter to sauté
20g	plain, low fat yoghurt
2 tsp	Nando's Lime & Coriander Marinade
	cracked black pepper
	salad leaves, fresh coriander and lime wedges to garnish

Hot Peri-Peri Sardinian Shrimp

5 15 4

Ingredients

350g	raw peeled shrimp (or prawns)
240g	pasta shells
1 jar	Nando's Hot Peri-Peri Marinade
	olive oil & butter for sautéing
1	bunch fresh basil leaves
	Parmesan
	crème fraiché

Method:

- Heat a little olive oil and butter in a wide sauté pan.
- Throw in the shrimp and stir fry for 2 minutes.
- Pour on the Marinade and allow to cook for 4-6 minutes.
- Cook the pasta shells according to packet instructions, drain well and add to the shrimp.
- Stir through the basil leaves & divide between 4 dishes.
- Garnish with freshly grated Parmesan and, if desired, a dollop of crème fraiché.

Sweet Peri-Peri Prawn Cocktail

Blend 2 tablespoons of Nando's Sweet Peri Peri sauce with ½ cup of mayonnaise (or Greek yoghurt as a low fat alternative). Add a squirt of lime/lemon juice, a grind of coarse black pepper and mix with 400g shelled, cooked prawns. Use as a lovely topping for Avocado Ritz, an exotic filling for sandwiches or baguettes.

Tuscan Chicken Parcels

Perfect with buttery jacket potatoes and a green salad.

15 **20** **4**

Ingredients

4	chicken breasts,
8	slices Parma Ham (Proscuito)
1	ball of Mozzarella cheese cut into 8 thin slices
8	large basil leaves
1 tbsp	olive oil
1 jar	Nando's Sun-Dried Tomato & Basil Marinade

Method:

- Quarter each piece of chicken to give 16 pieces in total.
- Lay 8 pieces on a board and top each one with a slice of cheese.
- Top each piece of cheese with a basil leaf & then another piece of chicken.
- Wrap each "sandwich" of chicken in a slice of Parma Ham.
- Heat the oil in a non-stick pan and sear each parcel on both sides.
- Place the parcels in a ovenproof dish, pour over the marinade and bake at 200°C for 20 minutes.

This recipe also works really well with our Roasted Reds Cooking Sauce.

Oriental Chicken Laksa

Method:

- Pour the Marinade, milk & stock into a pan.
- Bring to a simmer, then add chicken and cook gently for 7-8 minutes.
- Boil the noodles for 3 mins, drain & divide between 4 warm bowls.
- Stir the herbs & pepper into the chicken broth.
- Ladle the sauce over the noodles and top with slices of chicken.
- Scatter coriander sprigs & pepper strips to garnish.

This recipe works just as well with our Coconut, Lime & Coriander Cooking Sauce.

Ingredients

1 jar	Nando's Lime & Coriander Marinade
400ml	coconut milk (1 tin)
100ml	fresh chicken stock
4	chicken breasts, each cut into 4 diagonal slices
3	bunches of rice noodles
1	handful of fresh basil leaves, finely torn coriander leaves, roughly chopped
1/2	red pepper/capsicum, sliced into long, fine strips

Keep it in the family

Phil is one of the driving forces behind Nando's sauces in the UK. He knows how to keep the team happy and motivated with a relaxed attitude during the week and long lunches on a Friday.

Phil's own motivation is his family and it was a must that the office was located no further than 10 minutes from his home - getting back to help with the kids homework and helping make dinner is at least as important as hitting sales targets!

"The whole family loves Nando's, everytime we go to a Nando's for dinner the spice level we ask for seems to increase. Kate started really mild and now everything is medium at least. Claire and I have medium or hot depending on the occasion. John loves his Nando's plain chicken but even he wants to spice things up as he gets older.

At home we don't use Nando's all the time (honest) but one of our favourites is Roasted Red Chicken with Mozzarella & Basil. Simple to make, very tasty and everyone loves it, especially the stringy cheese........."

Phil, Claire, Kate & John

Roasted Red Chicken with Mozzarella & Basil

 10 20 4

Ingredients

- 500g chicken breast fillets
- 100g mozzarella, cut into slices
- 1 jar Nando's Roasted Reds Cooking Sauce
         fresh basil

Method:

- Slit a pocket into each of the chicken fillets and stuff with the mozzarella cheese and basil.
- Place chicken fillets in a flat dish and pour the cooking sauce over
- Bake for 20 mins at 200°C or until cooked thoroughly.

Serve with rice or with baby new potatoes and a green salad.

"This is one of the family favourites in our house - simple to make and delicious!"

Chicken Breast stuffed with Leek and Bacon

Ingredients

- 500g   chicken breast fillets
- 100g   cream cheese
- 2   leeks
- 250ml Nando's Sun-dried Tomato & Basil Marinade
         bacon rashers cooked (cut into small pieces)
- 10g   crushed garlic
- 15ml   olive oil

Method:

- Cut leek into small dice and fry off to soften.
- Mix leeks, cheese and bacon.
- Make a pocket in the back of each fillet and stuff with the leek, bacon and cheese mix.
- Hold together with cocktail stick if required.
- Sear chicken in a sauté pan on all sides.
- Place in oven on a middle shelf at 200°C to cook.
- Heat Marinade through and pour over the chicken after 10 minutes.
- Cook for at least another 10 minutes.

Honey Peanut Chicken Noodles

10 | 20 | 4

Ingredients

4	chicken fillets, skinned
300g	vermicelli
1 tbsp	olive oil
1 jar	Nando's Honey Peanut/Sesame Satay Cooking Sauce
1	bunch spring onions, thinly chopped/sliced
2 tbsp	chopped salted peanuts

Method:

· Preheat the oven to 180°C.

· Place the chicken in an ovenproof dish.

· Cover with the cooking sauce and oven bake for 20 minutes.

· Cook the pasta, drain, then toss with the olive oil and set aside.

· In a bowl mix the remaining ingredients, and add the vermicelli.

· When the chicken is cooked remove from the sauce and lightly toss the noodles in the remainder of the sauce.

· Slice the chicken and serve with the noodles.

Coconut Chicken Stir Fry

Ingredients

500g	diced chicken breast
1 jar	Nando's Lime & Coriander Marinade
1 tbsp	oil
1 clove	garlic, crushed
1 inch	ginger, grated
300g	ready-prepared stir-fry veg mix
300g	egg noodles, cooked
1 tin	coconut milk
1	bunch coriander, chopped

Method:

- Marinade the chicken in half of the marinade for at least 30 minutes.

- Heat a little oil in a wok or frying pan.

- Add the ginger, garlic & marinated chicken and stir-fry for 5 minutes.

- Add the vegetables and the noodles and stir fry for 3 minutes.

- Add the remaining marinade, coconut milk and coriander and stir thoroughly.

Beef Fillet with Peri-Peri Potato Latkes

This really is a very easy recipe, it only looks long!

Ingredients

500g	beef fillet (2 medium fillets)
1 jar	Nando's Roasted Reds Marinade
50g	rocket leaves
200g	cream cheese (1 tub)
500g	potatoes, washed and grated
1	egg
1 cup	cake flour
1 tsp	salt
2 tbsp	Nando's Medium Peri Peri
100ml	olive oil for frying

Method:

- Slice fillet lengthwise (don't cut through) and butterfly open. Flatten slightly with a meat hammer or rolling pin.

- Place in a flat dish and pour over Roasted Red Marinade. Allow to marinade for 25 minutes

- Preheat the grill.

- In the meanwhile, prepare the latkes.

- Grate the potatoes, and mix with the flour, salt, egg & Peri-Peri.

- Heat the oil in a deep frying pan, scoop spoonfuls of the latke mixture in the pan, flatten with a spatula and fry for 2 minutes on each side or until crisp and golden in colour.

- Remove from pan and drain excess oil on paper towel.

- Prepare the beef fillets as follows: - Remove from the marinade (don't wipe off excess marinade), place a thick layer of rocket leaves on one half of each fillet, fold the fillet over lengthwise to cover the leaves so the fillet returns to its original shape.

- Place fillet on a roasting rack and grill for 5 minutes. Turn over and grill the other side for 5 minutes.

- Place potato latkes on a serving dish and add a spoonful of cream cheese on to each.

- Slice fillets into medallions and place 2 medallions onto each potato latke.

- Serve hot.

Portuguese BBQ Steak with Zesty Rice

 10
 15
2

Ingredients

2	sirloin steaks
4-6 tbsp	Nando's Portuguese BBQ Marinade
1 cup	brown rice
1	bunch coriander leaves
1	lemon, zest and juice
2	spring onions, chopped

Method:

- Cook the rice according to packet instructions.
- In a bowl mix the coriander, lemon juice, zest and spring onions and mix into the rice. Keep warm.
- Slice the steak into finger width strips.
- Heat a little oil in a sauté pan and when very hot add the strips of meat.
- Turn and brown on all sides. (Alternatively grill or BBQ the steak.)
- Add the marinade and allow to bubble and sizzle for a couple of minutes until the meat is cooked as you like it.

Serve with a fresh green salad and the zesty rice

Mozzarella Meat Balls

Ingredients

500g	lean minced beef
2	spring onions, finely chopped
1 tbsp	dijon mustard
1 tbsp	Worcester sauce
2	cloves garlic
	fresh basil (torn)
1 tsp	dried basil
100g	mozzarella – 1/2 cut into cubes, the rest grated
2 jars	Nando's Sun-dried Tomato & Basil Marinade

Method:

• Mix all the ingredients together in a bowl with your hands (except the marinade and mozzarella).

• Roll the mixture into 12 medium sized or 24 mini balls, stuffing a cube of mozzarella into each one.

• Fry in a little vegetable oil (in batches to maintain the pan heat) to colour on all sides.

• Transfer the balls to an ovenproof dish big enough to fit them in a single layer.

• Pour over the marinade.

• Bake in 180°C oven for 20 minutes.

• Sprinkle top with remaining mozzarella and flash back in the oven to melt.

Roasted Red Meat Balls

Ingredients

500g	lean minced beef
1	garlic clove, crushed
1/2	onion, diced/finely chopped
1 tsp	fresh or dried thyme leaves
1/2	aubergine, diced
4 tbsp	olive oil
2 tbsp	plain flour mixed with lots of salt and pepper
1 jar	Nando's Roasted Reds Cooking Sauce
400g	spaghetti
1 ball	buffalo mozzarella torn or chopped into small chunks
1 bunch	parsley, washed and chopped

Method:

- Heat a little olive oil in a large pan.
- Add the aubergine and some salt and cook for 10 minutes. Set aside.
- Mix the mince, garlic, onion and thyme together and form into 16 balls.
- Roll in seasoned flour.
- Heat the remaining olive oil and fry the balls to colour all round.
- Remove to a paper towel to drain.
- Pour the jar of Roasted Reds plus 1/3 jar water into a saucepan.
- Heat and then add the meat balls and aubergine.
- Simmer gently for approximately 10 minutes.
- Meanwhile cook and drain the spaghetti then toss with a little olive oil, salt and pepper.
- Add 2/3 of the mozzarella and the parsley to the meatballs. Gently stir to mix.
- Divide the spaghetti between 4 bowls.
- Top with the meat balls and spoon over the sauce.
- Sprinkle over the remaining mozzarella.

Seafood Curry

10 / 15 / 4

Ingredients

3	spring onions, sliced into 1 inch lengths
300g	salmon, cubed into large pieces
200g	fresh prawns , peeled
1 jar	Nando's Curry Coconut Cooking Sauce
1 tbsp	sunflower oil
	coriander to garnish (chopped)

Method:

- Heat the oil in a sauté pan and add the spring onions to brown.

- Add the salmon and prawns.

- Shake the pan about to seal the seafood and colour everything nicely.

- Add the cooking sauce, reduce the heat and allow the pan to cook over a gentle heat for 5 minutes by which time the fish and prawns should be perfectly cooked.

- Serve with rice and scatter with chopped coriander.

Thai Prawn Noodles

 15 **10**  **2**

Ingredients

20	king prawns, peeled & cooked
2 tbsp	Nando's Sweet Peri-Peri Sauce
4	bunches rice noodles

Dressing Ingredients

2	limes, juice & zest
1 tbsp	thai fish sauce
2 tbsp	raw cane caster sugar
1	red chilli, deseeded and finely sliced
1	bunch mint, finely shredded (small handful)
1	bunch coriander, chopped
1 tbsp	olive oil
1/2	cucumber, deseeded and cut into matchsticks (3 inch)
1	spring onion, finely sliced
4 tbsp	peanuts, chopped

This dish is also great as a starter (serves 4)

Method:

- Mix the dressing ingredients together in a bowl.
- Cook the noodles, rinse in cold water, drain thoroughly and add to the bowl of dressing.
- In a separate bowl mix the prawns with the Peri-Peri.
- Serve a mound of noodles on each plate, top with the prawns and garnish with mint.

Lime & Coriander Fish Cakes

Another Nando's dad says "I made it with Matthew my 3 year old son, we had great fun mixing all the ingredients together, getting messy and then forming lots of different shaped fishcakes. Matthew couldn't decide what's best - eating the shapes when cooked or making them in the first place"

Method:

- Soak the white bread in the cream for about 10 minutes and then mash with your hands.

- Place the fish and bread mix in a bowl.

- Add the onion, fresh coriander & Lime and Coriander Marinade mixing thoroughly. Season with salt and pepper.

To form the Fish Cakes:

- With wet hands divide the mixture into fish cakes (approx 6-8 cakes) and roll in flour.

- Place on a tray with grease proof paper. Refrigerate and allow to chill for 1 hour.

- Remove from the fridge & coat in egg and roll in the bread crumbs.

- Shallow fry and serve with Nando's Curry Coconut Cooking Sauce as a dipping sauce.

Ingredients

500g	shredded white fish, filleted and cooked (skin off)
100ml	cream
6	slices of white bread, crusts removed, and crumbed
1	bunch fresh coriander, chopped
1/2	medium onion, diced into 1 cm squares
1/2 jar	Nando's Lime & Coriander Marinade
	Nando's Curry Coconut Cooking Sauce (to serve as a dip)
1 tsp	lemon juice
1	egg
2	crusty rolls broken into bread crumbs
1	handful of flour
	veg/sunflower oil for shallow frying
	sea salt and cracked black pepper for seasoning

Zanzibar Fish Fingers

Ingredients

200g	firm white fish (e.g. cod or kingclip) cut into 2 inch strips
1/2 jar	Nando's Fresh Lemon Cooking Sauce
2 tbsp	fresh parsley
1/2 tsp	black pepper

Method:

- Preheat the oven to 180°C
- Mix together the Cooking Sauce with the parsley and pepper.
- Toss fish in the Cooking Sauce to coat well.
- Place on a baking tray and roast until caramelised (approx 10 minutes).

Serve with potato waffles or chips and peas.

This recipe works just as well with our Coconut, Lime & Coriander Cooking Sauce.

Spicy Lamb Tagine

 30 30 4

Ingredients

¼ tsp	salt
½ tsp	black pepper
½ tsp	ground cumin
½ tsp	ground coriander
4	trimmed lamb fillets
2 tbsp	olive oil
1	small butternut pumpkin/squash, peeled and cubed
2	parsnips, cut into batons
2	carrots, cut into batons
1	red onion, cut into 16 thin wedges
4 cloves	garlic
1 jar	Nando's Curry Coconut Cooking Sauce
2	tomatoes, quartered
12	ready-to-eat prunes or figs, cut in half
400g	chick peas, drained (1 tin)
3 tbsp	thick greek yoghurt
1 tbsp	chopped mint + few sprigs for garnish
1 tbsp	chopped coriander + few sprigs for garnish

Serve with couscous or rice.

Method:

- Mix together the salt, pepper and spices with 2 tsp of oil, rub this mixture into the lamb and set aside.

- Heat 2 tsp of oil in a large non-stick pan and sauté the butternut, parsnips, carrots and onion, along with the garlic, for 5 minutes. Shake about so they don't catch.

- Add the Curry Coconut Cooking Sauce, ½ cup water, tomatoes, fruit and chick peas and simmer for 20-25 minutes.

- Mix the yoghurt and chopped herbs and set aside.

- Meanwhile grill, BBQ or pan fry the spicy lamb.

- Divide the stew between 4 warmed bowls, then slice the lamb on the diagonal and add to the stew.

- Top each bowl with a dollop of the yoghurt and some sprigs of coriander & mint.

Roasted Red Pasta Salad

Ingredients

250g **tagliatelle**

2 tbsp **olive oil**

80g **feta cheese, diced**

1/2 jar **Nando's Roasted Reds Marinade**

1 **red pepper/capsicum, roasted and sliced into strips**

1 **yellow pepper/capsicum, roasted and sliced into strips**

Method:

- Cook the pasta according to packet instructions.

- Drain and toss in a large bowl with the olive oil

- Add the remaining ingredients and serve.

Peri Hot Pot!

Ingredients

1 tbsp	olive oil
1	onion, chopped
3	cloves garlic, crushed
1/4	aubergine, washed and diced
1 tbsp	dried oregano
2	carrots, peeled and chopped
2	parsnips, peeled and chopped
1	sweet potato, peeled and chopped
1	red pepper/capsicum, washed and chopped
2	leeks, washed and sliced
1	bulb fennel, washed and sliced
1 jar	Nando's Sun-dried Tomato & Basil Marinade
	few drops of soy sauce

Method:

- Heat the oil in a large pan and sauté the onion and garlic until soft

- Add the aubergine and oregano.

- Stir around for a few minutes and then add all the other vegetables.

- Pour in the marinade and add about 300mls water and the soy sauce.

- Bring to a boil and simmer for 20-30 minutes until the vegetables are tender.

Serve with
steamed brown rice

Curry Coconut Risotto

Ingredients

250ml	Arborio rice
50g	butter
2 cloves	garlic, crushed
50g	chopped onion
1 jar	Nando's Curry Coconut Cooking Sauce
425g	coconut milk (1 can)
1	head of Bok Choy, chopped

Method:

- Melt the butter in a large pan and lightly fry the onions and garlic.
- Add rice and stir through making sure it is well coated by the butter.
- Combine the cooking sauce and coconut milk (to make 1 1/2 pints of liquid).
- On a moderate heat, add a small amount of the liquid to the rice at a time – evaporate the liquid and repeat until completely absorbed.
- Stir often to prevent the rice from sticking to the bottom of the pot.
- Remove from the heat and stir the Bok Choy through the rice.

Option: add diced, stir-fried chicken along with the cooking sauce.

Nando's Potato Curry

A hot and aromatic potato curry, excellent with poppadums and Basmati rice.

 15 25 4

Ingredients

2 tbsp	sunflower oil
2 cloves	fresh garlic, crushed
1	medium onion, sliced
1	medium green pepper/capsicum, cut into strips
2	medium potato, washed, peeled and cut into chunks
2 cups	cauliflower pieces
1 tsp	cumin
1 tsp	salt
½ tsp	whole mustard seeds
1 jar	Nando's Curry Coconut Cooking Sauce
250g	button mushrooms
1 tbsp	fresh coriander

Method:

- Heat oil then fry garlic and onions til glossy.

- Add pepper/capsicum, potato, cauliflower, cumin, salt, mustard seeds cooking sauce and 2/3 cup water and bring to the boil. Simmer for 15 minutes.

- Add button mushrooms and coriander and simmer for 2 minutes.

Serve with Basmati rice and freshly chopped coriander.

Girls just want to have fun!

Rosi is from Portugal originally and has grown up enjoying the taste sensation of Peri-Peri, so it's no wonder that she spices up a night in with Nando's Peri-Peri!

Rosi now works at the Nando's head office in Putney, London and often invites her work 'family' round to catch up on the gossip they hear at the office – it's too busy to chat during the day!

"When the girls come round we don't want to be cooking, just talking! The easiest thing is to jazz up some plain dips with Peri-Peri and grab some tortilla chips, and if we want more to eat the Club Sandwiches are a breeze to make while we chat, then just flash under the grill. Then all we need is a bottle (or two) of wine, and bring on the gossip!"

Nando's Club Sandwich

10 | **25** | **2**

Ingredients
(Per Sandwich)

3	**pieces toast**
2	**slices cheese**
2	**slices cooked chicken breast tossed with**
1 tbsp	**Nando's Lemon & Rosemary Marinade**
2	**pieces cooked streaky bacon**
8	**slices tomato**
100ml	**mayonnaise mixed with**
2 tbsp	**Nando's Lemon & Rosemary Marinade**
4	**cocktail sticks**

Method:

- Preheat the oven to 180°C
- Make the sandwiches in this order, starting with a slice of toast:
- Toast
- Mayonnaise
- Bacon
- 4 slices of tomato
- Cheese
- Toast
- Mayonnaise
- Chicken
- 4 slices of tomato
- Cheese
- Mayonnaise
- Toast
- Then slice off the crusts, if desired, and insert 4 cocktail sticks to keep it together.
- Pop the sandwich onto a baking tray and cook in the oven for 5-10 minutes until the cheese looks runny.
- Cut into four and enjoy warm.

Chicken & Lime Kebabs with Mango Salsa

10 10 2

Ingredients

2 **chicken breasts, cubed**

2 **limes, sliced**

1/2 jar **Nando's Curry Coconut Cooking Sauce**

6 **skewers/kebab sticks (wet)**

Salsa Ingredients

1 **mango, peeled and cubed (or tinned)**

1 **lime, zest and juice**

small bunch coriander, finely chopped

1 tbsp **Nando's Medium Peri-Peri sauce**

Method:

- Place chunks of chicken in a bowl and smother with the cooking sauce.

- Thread chunks of chicken onto each bamboo skewer and alternate with slices of lime. Allow 2 slices lime per skewer.

- Place on a baking sheet and grill for approximately 10 minutes, turning regularly.

- Meanwhile mix the salsa ingredients together.

- Serve hot or cold.

Peri-Peri Artichoke Dip

Ingredients

- 1 can   tinned artichoke hearts
- 1/3 jar   Nando's Fresh Lemon Cooking Sauce
- 1-2 tbsp   Nando's Medium or Hot Peri-Peri Sauce
- 1 tub   low-fat cream cheese
-   chopped parsley to garnish

Method:

- Whizz the artichokes in a food processor until roughly chopped
- Add the remaining ingredients and puree until smooth
- Pour into a serving bowl and serve with pitta and crudité

Prawn Tortilla Chips

Ingredients

- 250g   prawns
- 1 large   bag tortilla chips (nachos)
- 1   mango, chopped into small dice
- 1   paw paw, chopped into small dice (or tinned)
- 1   lime, zest and juice
- 1   small bunch coriander
- 3   spring onions, finely chopped
- 1   small pot of greek yoghurt
- 4 tbsp   Nando's Lime & Coriander Marinade

Method:

- Chop half the prawns, mix with half the marinade and set aside.
- Mix the fruit with the lime juice and zest.
- Add the spring onions and the coriander to the fruit. Season with salt and pepper.
- Mix the remaining marinade into the yoghurt.
- Onto each tortilla put a pile of chopped marinated prawns.
- Top with a mound of fruit salsa, a whole prawn and a dollop of yoghurt.
- Garnish with coriander.

White Chocolate, Lime and Peri-Peri Mousse

+ 2 hours cooling time

Ingredients

500 g	white chocolate
500 ml	cream
5	egg whites
5	gelatine leaves, soaked
100 ml	fresh lime juice
250 g	caster sugar
2 tbsp	Nando's Sweet Peri-Peri Sauce

Method:

- Melt chocolate in a bowl over a pan of gently simmering water, then keep warm.
- Whip cream to ribbon consistency.
- Heat lime juice, caster sugar and Peri-Peri over low heat then allow to cool slightly.
- Add soaked gelatine leaves and stir to dissolve.
- Whip egg whites until they form soft peaks (meringue).
- When cool, carefully fold chocolate into the cream, gently stir in lime mixture and lightly add egg whites using a metal spoon.
- Spoon into lightly greased moulds and chill for at least two hours in fridge.

Chilli Rum Sauce for Ice Cream

Ingredients

1 1/2 cups	sugar
1/2 cup	water
1/2 cup	rum
1	fresh chilli, finely sliced
1/2	pineapple, cut into small cubes
1 tsp	Nando's Hot Peri-Peri Sauce

Method:

- Boil the sugar and water until the sugar is dissolved, then simmer* for another 15 minutes.
- Add the remaining ingredients and boil for 1 minute.
- Pour into a sealable bottle and chill.
- Best used the next day to allow flavour to develop (use within a week).

* If boiled, liquid will turn to toffee.

Nando's Peri-Meri –
the perfect alternative to a Bloody Mary!

Ingredients

800g	tomato juice
1 tsp	celery salt
1 tbsp	Worcestershire sauce
	few twists of black pepper
1 tbsp	Nando's Medium Peri Peri sauce
1	fresh lime, juiced
4	shots vodka
4	sticks celery, trimmed, to garnish

Method:

- Make the Peri-Meri mixture by mixing all ingredients together except for the vodka.
- When ready to serve, fill each glass to the top with ice cubes.
- Add a generous shot of vodka.
  - Pour over the Peri-Meri mixture.
  - Rub the fleshy side of the squeezed lime shell around the rim of each glass.
  - Add a stick of celery and serve.

Mango Peri-Lassi
Ingredients

250g	ripe mango
250ml	chilled coconut milk
250ml	yoghurt
4	shots of vodka
1 tsp	Nando's Sweet Peri-Peri Sauce

Method:

- Blend all the ingredients together in a blender adding 8 ice cubes.
- Served chilled with spicy snacks.

see page 69 for spicy nuts & olives.

Goal !!

A meal of two halves

Craig works closely with the Nando's team in South Africa, working on the website, new designs and adverts and generally putting in a lot of hours – we think it's just to make sure he gets plenty of free meals at the local Nando's!

"This is my house. This is my telly. These are my mates. They live here on Saturdays and Sundays (and during the week) whenever there is a big game on or while we warm up for a night out. It's not my company that brings them here and it's certainly not the ladies. No, no, no, NO it's the delicious spread I lay on with my endless supply of Nando's sauces.

Every week I notice how fast my snacks, chicken wings, sandwiches and what ever they can get their hands on, disappear before the whistle has even gone for kick-off.

So this is how I have won my friends over. By creating the most delicious spicy dips, cooking up the hottest meatballs, and always having a jar of Peri-Peri sauce on hand for extra spice and flavour, I have made sure that I never watch the game alone. So thanks to Nando's I am the most popular guy in the neighbourhood.

You too can become "one of the boys" with Nando's."

offside !!

Craig

free kick ...

Half-time

Referee!!

The final whistle

The Nando's Hangover Fillet

Ingredients

1.5kg	beef fillet
1 jar	Nando's Hot Peri-Peri sauce
120g	anchovy fillets (1 can), finely chopped
3 tbsp	capers
2 tbsp	tomato paste
3 tbsp	pitted black olives, minced
2 tsp	garlic (crushed)
1 tsp	salt
1 tsp	crushed black pepper
1 jar	Nando's Roasted Reds Cooking Sauce
	olive oil

Method:

- Blend together the Hot Peri-Peri Sauce, anchovy fillets, capers, tomato paste, garlic, salt, black pepper and olives.

- Cut the fillet into 6 equal portions.

- Turn each piece to stand up, and cut a slit in the side of the fillet. Using a teaspoon, spoon some of the filling into each fillet. Use a toothpick to pin the pocket closed again.

- Heat a little olive oil in a thick based pan and sear the fillets to brown in the pan.

- Remove from pan, and pour the Nando's Roasted Reds Cooking Sauce into the pan. Heat through.

- Now place the fillets back in the pan and simmer for 10 minutes or until the steak is cooked to your liking.

Perfect with Hot Wedges (page 48)

Ingredients

500g	lamb mince
3 tsp	crushed cumin
3 cloves	crushed garlic
1 tsp	salt
1 tsp	black pepper
125ml	Nando's Portuguese BBQ Marinade
1	egg
1/2 cup	bread crumbs
8	kebab skewers
2 cups	steamed couscous (prepared according to manufacturers instructions)

Dressing Ingredients

30ml	fresh coriander, finely chopped
250ml	greek yoghurt
100g or 1/4	cucumber
1 clove	crushed garlic
50ml	Nando's Lime & Coriander Marinade

Lamb Kofta on Couscous

 20   10   4

Method:

- Blend all ingredients for kofta together to uniform consistency and divide into 8.
- Shape into firm casings around skewers (about 10-12cm long sausages).
- Pre-heat oven to 180°C.
- Cook at the top of the oven for 10 minutes, turning once.
- Prepare the dressing by blending all dressing ingredients together in food processor.
- Prepare couscous according to packet instructions.
- Serve the kofta's on couscous and pour over the dressing.

Soccer Meat-Balls

20 | **25** | **4**

Method:

- Mix all the ingredients together in a bowl with your hands (except the marinade and mozzarella).

- Roll the mixture into 12 medium sized or 24 mini balls, stuffing a cube of mozzarella into each one.

- Fry in a little vegetable oil to colour on all sides.

- Transfer the balls to an ovenproof dish, big enough to accommodate them in a single layer.

- Pour over 2 jars of the Marinade.

- Bake in 180°C oven for 20 minutes.

- Sprinkle top with remaining mozzarella and flash back in the oven to melt.

Ingredients

500g	lean minced beef
1	red onion
1 tbsp	Dijon mustard
1 tbsp	Worcester sauce
2 cloves	crushed garlic
50g	jalapenos
1	red chilli
100g	mozzarella – 1/2 cut into cubes, the rest grated
2 jars	Nando's Sun-dried Tomato & Basil Marinade

Smokey BBQ Potatoes

Ingredients

300g	**new potatoes**
2-3 tbsp	**olive oil**
25g	**butter**
3 tbsp	**Nando's Smokey BBQ Marinade**

Method:

- Cover the potatoes with cold water, add a little salt and cook until tender.
- Drain and slice into 5mm rounds.
- Heat the olive oil and butter in a frying pan.
- Add the sliced potatoes and fry on both sides until golden.
- Coat potatoes with the Marinade and cook on a low heat to warm through.
- Garnish with fresh herbs and serve immediately.

Hot Wedges

Ingredients

2 or 3	**large baking potatoes, washed**
1/2 jar	**Nando's Hot Peri-Peri Marinade**
1 tbsp	**olive oil**

Method:

- Cut each potato into wedges.
- Parboil the wedges for 10 minutes.
- Mix the oil and marinade together in a large bowl.
- Drain the potatoes, tip into the bowl and stir gently.
- Set aside for 15 minutes whilst you pre-heat the oven to 200°C.
- Roast the potatoes in a non-stick baking tray for 40 minutes, turning every 15 minutes.
- Serve with a sour cream dip (and maybe a bit of Peri-Peri!).

Flash Fried Olives & Feta

Ingredients

- 200g **black olives**
- 50g **feta cheese – cubed**
- 1 tbsp **olive oil**
- 1/2 tsp **sea salt**
- 1/2 jar **Nando's Medium Peri-Peri Sauce**

Method:

- Heat the olive oil in a sauté pan over a high heat.
- Add the olives and toss until hot.
- Pour on the Peri-Peri and toss to coat the olives.
- When bubbling, add the feta and season with salt.
- Serve immediately.

ilk
Tea bags
sugar
biscuits

Let us entertain you!

Entertaining friends and family is the best way to show off your favourite recipes or try out something new... or you could enjoy letting someone else entertain you!

Charlotte from Nando's South Africa is a big fan of having people round for dinner, especially as her girlfriends help out with the preparation! Husband Johan loves to braai, so a typical meal would include the Layered Polenta Cake served with barbecued meats and a fresh salad. Another favourite is Chicken Potjie, a delicious chicken casserole cooked in a cast iron pot inside the braai, and served with freshly baked bread. And thanks to the clever layout of their house the easy-going evening often rounds up with a dip in the adjoining jacuzzi!

Keit from the Nando's team loves to be entertained at her friends' but will get stuck into the cooking at boyfriend Lesiba's house when it comes round to their turn! Depending on the mood of the day Keit's friends will stoke up the braai or cook indoors, enjoying simple and delicious meals with lots of fresh locally grown veggies.

Layered Polenta Cake with Roasted Reds & Mozzarella

Ingredients

250g	raw polenta
250g	cream cheese
30ml	olive oil
30ml	garlic
200g	onions sliced (1 medium sized)
600g	chicken fillets cut into small cubes (1cm diced)
20g	fresh oregano & basil (mixed)
	salt
	coarse black pepper
1 jar	Nando's Roasted Reds Cooking Sauce
175g	grated mozzarella cheese
1	green pepper/capsicum sliced into strips
1	red pepper/capsicum sliced into strips

25 **20** **6**

Method:

- Pre-heat the oven to 180°C.

- Roast peppers/capsicum in a little oil in the oven until charred.

- Prepare polenta according to manufacturers instructions. While polenta is still warm, blend with cream cheese until consistent texture. Spoon polenta into a loose bottomed cake tin and smooth down. Refrigerate to set.

- In a saucepan, heat olive oil then fry garlic and onions until translucent. Add the chicken and fry until brown. Add the salt, oregano, basil, black pepper and cooking sauce. Allow to simmer for 5 minutes.

- Once the polenta has set, transfer the polenta base from the cake tin to an ovenproof serving dish.

- Spoon the chicken and sauce onto the base and sprinkle with the mozzarella cheese. Arrange the green and red pepper/capsicum strips on top of the cheese.

- Bake for 15 minutes or until cheese is crisp and brown.

Butternut Curry Soup

Ingredients

1kg	butternuts (or 1kg ready peeled and cut into cubes)
1 litre	water
2 tsp	salt
1/2 jar	Nando's Curry Coconut Cooking Sauce
50g	butter or oil
400ml	coconut milk (1 can)
	freshly chopped coriander leaves
	salt to taste

Method:

- Peel and deseed the butternut and cut into 1 inch cubes.

- Place into a medium sized pan with the water and salt and bring to the boil.

- Reduce heat and simmer for 25 minutes or until butternut is soft.

- Drain the butternut, and keep the drained liquid. Place the butternut in a food processor and blend to smooth. Add some drained liquid back if puree is too thick.

- Pour back into the pot and heat up again slowly, stirring to prevent burning. Add the Cooking Sauce and coconut milk, stir and heat through until hot.

Serve with freshly chopped coriander and fresh crusty rolls

Chickpea & Butternut Samosas

Ingredients

50ml	sunflower oil
2 cloves	fresh garlic, crushed
2	medium onion, sliced
1kg	butternut chunks
2 tins	chickpeas
2 cups	boiled lentils
1 tsp	salt
1 Jar	Nando's Morrocan Curry Cooking Sauce
	fresh coriander leaves
	melted butter
1	pack filo pastry

Method:

- Boil butternut in salted water for 10 minutes.
- Heat oil then fry garlic and onions till glossy. Add lentils, chickpeas, butternut and cooking sauce and bring to the boil. Simmer for 10 minutes. Season to taste. Leave to cool completely.
- Unfold filo pastry and cover with damp cloth. (do not let pastry dry out).
- Cut pastry into 10cm wide strips.
- Layer 3 strips on top of each other and brush top layer with melted butter.

- Spoon a tablespoon of butternut mixture on the bottom corner (about 5 cms/2" from the end). Fold corner diagonally across to cover filling (forming a triangle). Roll corner across (right to left) and continue to end of pastry strip. Fold the end and brush the top with melted butter to seal.
- Repeat until all strips are filled and rolled into triangular samosa shapes.
- Place on a lightly oiled baking tray at the top of a preheated oven at 200°C. Bake for approximately 10 minutes (dependent on size of parcels).

Nando's Tuscan Lentils

 15 6/8

as a
side dish

Ingredients

1/2 cup	puy lentils
6	cloves garlic, unpeeled
1	bunch of fresh thyme
3 tbsp	olive oil
2 tsp	Nando's Hot Peri-Peri Sauce
3 tsp	mixed herbs
400g	borlotti beans (1 tin)
175g	chickpeas

Method:

- Boil the lentils in plenty of water for 15 minutes (or until soft) with the garlic cloves and a few sprigs of thyme but do not add any salt.

- Drain the lentils in a sieve over a bowl, reserving some of the cooking liquid. Pick out the thyme stalks, and chop the leaves. Discard the stripped stalks.

- Peel the garlic cloves and put them into a wide bowl.

- Crush the garlic with a fork and add the oil and Peri-Peri.

- Add the hot lentils, borlotti beans, chickpeas and chopped thyme leaves.

- Allow to cool, then taste for seasoning and serve at room temperature.

- Excellent the following day once the flavours have developed and wonderful as a salad.

Stuffed Sun-dried Tomato Peppers

 20 **30** **6**

Ingredients

6	red peppers/capsicums
450g	beef mince
1	medium onion, finely diced
1 tsp	salt
1 tsp	black pepper
1/2 jar	Nando's Sun-dried Tomato & Basil Marinade
300g	buffalo mozzarella cheese

Method:

- Preheat the oven to 180°C.
- Cut the tops off the peppers/capsicum and remove seeds and white veins.
- Blend the mince, onion, salt, pepper and Marinade together in a mixing bowl. Allow to stand for 10 minutes.
- Scoop the mince mixture into the pepper/capsicum and place into an ovenproof baking dish. Drizzle with a little olive oil.
- Bake for 30 minutes.
- 5 minutes from the end of cooking, melt a little cheese over the top of each pepper/capsicum.

The peppers can also be wrapped in foil and placed in between medium hot coals of BBQ for 10 minutes

Zingy Roasted Vegetables

 **15** **40** **4**

Ingredients

1 jar	Nando's Fresh Lemon Cooking Sauce
2	packs of ready to roast Mediterranean vegetables

(or prepare your own - chunks of red onion, courgette, aubergine, pepper/capsicum and sweet potato.)

Method:

- Pre-heat the oven to 220°C.
- Place the vegetables onto a roasting tray, lightly coat in olive oil and cook vegetables for 15 minutes. Pour over the cooking sauce and return to oven.
- Roast for 25 minutes, basting regularly.
- Serve with rice and chicken.

Brinjal Bakes

The Brinjal is native to India and is a familiar component of Indian curries. It is known as Malayan Purple Melon in China where it has been a common food item since 600 BC.

English speakers named it Eggplant, maybe due to the shape of first varieties they came across, and it still has this name in Australia.

In the UK Aubergine is the common name for Brinjal.

Brinjal is considered to have medicinal properties even though none of these properties have any scientific base. In a few countries in Africa the brinjal is used as medicine to treat epilepsy and convulsions. In South East Asia it is still used to treat stomach cancer and measles.

Ingredients

- **2**   **medium sized aubergines (brinjals), cut diagonally into 1/4 inch scallop slices,**
- **1**   **large onion, sliced finely into rings**
- **2**   **large, ripe tomatoes cut into 1/4 inch slices**
- **200g**   **grated mozzarella cheese**
- **1 jar**   **Nando's Sun-dried Tomato & Basil Marinade**
- **50ml**   **olive oil**
-    **sea salt and cracked black pepper to taste**

Method:

- Preheat oven to 200°C.
- In an oven proof dish, start with an aubergine slice for the base of each stack, ensuring that the slices don't overlap or touch each other.
- Place a slice of onion rings onto each auberguine slice.
- In a bowl, mix the cheese and 200ml of the Marinade together (saving 2-4 tablespoons of Marinade as a topping).
- Place a spoonful of this mixture onto each stack.
- Add a slice of tomato to each stack, and season with sea salt and cracked black pepper.
- Keep adding layers until the ingredients are all used, then drizzle with olive oil and the remainder of the marinade.
- Bake in a preheated oven for 15 - 20 minutes or until cheese has melted and crisped.
- Allow to stand for approximately 5 mins before serving.

Serve with a crisp green salad
& garlic bread.

Chicken with Spinach & Prawns

Method:

- Lightly grease an ovenproof dish. Preheat the oven to 180°C.

- Cut a pocket into the top of each chicken breast.

- Microwave the spinach for 3 minutes and roughly chop.

- Take half the spinach and shape into 4 piles in the baking dish.

- Mix the remaining spinach with the prawns, salt & pepper and stuff this mixture inside the chicken breasts.

- Place each stuffed chicken breast onto a pile of spinach.

- Pour over the cooking sauce and bake for 30 minutes or until thoroughly cooked.

- Garnish with sprigs of coriander.

Perfect served with rice mixed with chopped coriander and lemon zest.

Ingredients

4	chicken breasts, skinned
1 bag	spinach (225g)
160g	prawns, peeled and chopped
1 jar	Nando's Curry Coconut Cooking Sauce
	sea salt & cracked black pepper
	fresh coriander to garnish

Basil & Parmesan Chicken on Lemon Couscous

Ingredients

500g	skinless chicken fillets (4)
1 jar	Nando's Sun-dried Tomato & Basil Marinade
50g	(¹/4 cup) bread crumbs
50g	(¹/4 cup) parmesan cheese
20g	(¹/4 cup) freshly chopped basil leaves
1	cup dried couscous
1	lemon
30g	pitted black olives, coarsely chopped
	parsley, coarsely chopped
	sea salt to season

Method:

- Marinate chicken in the marinade for 25 minutes, saving a little marinade for serving.

- Mix bread crumbs, parmesan cheese and freshly chopped basil together.

- Preheat oven to 180°C.

- Remove chicken fillets from the marinade and roll in the crumb mixture.

- Place on an roasting rack and bake for 30 minutes.

- Meanwhile prepare the couscous according to manufacturer's instruction. Season to taste. Stir in the grated rind of one lemon, the olives and the parsley.

- Spoon couscous into a flat serving dish, and place the chicken on top. Drizzle with the marinade set aside.

Ingredients

500g beef fillet

1 jar Nando's Portuguese BBQ Marinade

5 medium potatoes, cooked, peeled and sliced in rounds

olive oil to shallow fry

2 tbsp Nando's Garlic (or Hot) Peri-Peri Sauce

300g fresh / frozen raspberries

2 tbsp Nando's Sweet Peri-Peri Sauce

salad leaves to serve

1 ripe avocado

Avocado Preparation:

1. To remove the avocado stone, using the point of a sharp knife cut the avocado circumference in half lengthways and twist to separate.

2. Carefully chop diagonally into the stone and twist the knife releasing the stone.

3. Peel back the skin from each half, lay cut side down and slice lengthways.

Beef Fillet with Sweet Raspberry Salad

Method:

- Halve the fillet lengthwise into 2 strips.

- Place in a dish, pour over the marinade and allow to marinate overnight (covered, in the fridge).

- Blend the raspberries and sieve to remove the seeds.

- Stir in the Sweet Peri-Peri Sauce and refrigerate.

- Heat olive oil in shallow frying pan, and fry potato slices till golden. Add the Garlic Peri-Peri and fry until absorbed.

- Divide the fried potatoes onto 4 plates.

- Heat the pan again, and sear the marinated fillet all around for approximately 1 minute on each side, 4 minutes in total – to serve rare (Cook longer if desired).

- Remove fillet from pan and slice into 5-7mm thick slices.

- Fan slices of fillet on top of the fried potatoes and top with salad leaves.

- Prepare the avocado (see tip) and place on the salad leaves, then dress with the raspberry dressing.

1.

2.

3.

Lime and Coriander Salmon with a Roasted Pepper/Capsicum Salad

Ingredients

4	salmon fillets (skinned)
100 ml	Nando's Lime and Coriander Marinade
100 g	butter
80 ml	cream
	juice from 1 lemon
1 cup	dried bulgar wheat
1/2	red pepper/capsicum
1/2	green pepper/capsicum
1/2	yellow pepper/capsicum
60 ml	olive oil
	sea salt & cracked black pepper

Method:

- Cook bulgar wheat to manufacturer's instructions.
- Stir with a fork to loosen granules.
- Cut peppers into 2cm chunks and sauté in olive oil in a hot pan. Season with salt and pepper.
- When cool, mix peppers/capsicum into the bulgar wheat.
- Mix the marinade, butter, cream and lemon juice in sauté pan and heat through gently.
- Stir consistently until it thickens and to ensure it does not split, keep warm.
- Sear salmon in a hot pan until it browns evenly.
- Serve the salmon on a bed of bulgar wheat and drizzle over the sauce.

Fish Roasted in a Foil Packet

Ingredients

1 1/4 cups	rice
2 tbsp	toasted pine nuts (bake on a tray for 3-5 minutes in a 180°C oven)
1	lemon, juice and zest
	chopped mixed herbs such as parsley, chives and dill
6 tbsp	Nando's Lime & Coriander Marinade
200g	peeled king prawns
250g	skinless salmon fillet, cut into largish pieces
200g	sea bass fillet (or fleshy chunky white fish), cut into largish pieces
4	squares kitchen foil, buttered

Method:

- Divide the fish and prawns equally between the foil squares.
- Spoon 1/2 tbsp of marinade over each pile of fish and prawns.
- Tightly seal each foil package and bake for 10 minutes or until cooked in a 180°C oven.
- Cook the rice then stir in the remaining marinade, lemon juice, lemon rind, pine nuts and herbs.
- Place a mound of rice on each warmed plate and top with a pile of fish and prawns.
- Scatter fresh herbs to garnish.

Pineapple & Peri-Peri Parfait

20 45 12+

Method:

- Place the pineapple in a blender and blend to a pulp.

- Place the pineapples and the chillies in a pan and simmer until the pineapples are soft.
  (Not required if using tinned pineapples)

Making the Stock Syrup

- Pour sugar and water into a saucepan and heat gently to dissolve sugar (test the sugar has dissolved using a wooden spoon - not metal).

- Bring to the boil and bubble for 5 mins without stirring.

- Take off heat and set aside.

- Meanwhile, using an electric mixer, whisk the egg yolks until ribbon stage.

- In a separate bowl, whip the cream to a similar consistency.

- Return the stock syrup to a high heat, add the vanilla pod and reduce the liquid down to 175ml.

- Set the mixer on slow speed and carefully drizzle the hot stock syrup into the egg mixture (avoiding the beaters and bowl) and continue whisking until cool.

- Fold the pineapples, chilli and Peri-Peri sauce into the egg mixture.

- Then gently fold in the cream mixture and pour into a 2 litre terrine mould lined with cling film.

- Freeze overnight then remove from the mould and serve in slices.

Ingredients

200ml	water
130g	sugar (to make 200 ml stock syrup)
1	vanilla pod, halved
500ml	double cream
2	pineapples (or use tinned pineapple)
3	red chillies, finely chopped
8	egg yolks
1 tbsp	Nando's Sweet Peri-Peri Sauce

This parfait is a bit of a challenge to make but it's definitely worth it!

Nando's Famous Peri-Peri Chocolate Sauce

Ingredients

75g	dark chocolate
150ml	double cream
1½ tsp	Nando's Medium Peri-Peri Sauce (or to taste)
1 tbsp	dark rum (optional)

Method:

- Heat everything together in a non-stick pan, except the rum, until the chocolate is melted.
- Add the rum and serve.

Serve with grilled pineapple slices, fruit skewers or barbecued bananas

Whisky Peri-Peri Sorbet

Ingredients

500g	sugar
1½ litres	water
40ml	lemon juice
150ml	whisky
1 tsp	Nandos Sweet Peri-Peri, strained through a fine sieve
2	egg whites

Method:

- Pour water, sugar and whisky into a large pan.
- Bring to boil for 5 minutes until sugar is dissolved.
- Add lemon juice and the Sweet Peri-Peri sauce.
- Cool to room temperature.
- Whisk through egg whites.
- Churn in an ice-cream machine until set.

Peri-Peri Olives

Ingredients

1 jar	Nando's Roasted Reds Cooking Sauce
1 tbsp	capers
2	cloves garlic
	zest of 1 lemon
1 tin	anchovies
2 tsp	marjoram
3 tsp	parsley
2 tsp	rosemary
4 tbsp	red wine vinegar
8 tbsp	olive oil
450g	mixed pitted olives, cracked slightly with the side of a rolling pin.

Method:

- Blend everything (except the olives) in a food processor until smooth.
- Place the mixture into a bag or plastic box.
- Add the olives and toss in the paste.
- Allow to mature for up to a week.

Peri-Peri Nuts

Ingredients

200g	mixed nuts – pecans, walnuts, almonds, brazils
4 tbsp	Nando's Hot Peri-Peri Sauce
	sprig rosemary, chopped
2 tbsp	olive oil
	pinch sugar
	pinch salt

Method:

- Mix everything together and spread the nuts out on a baking sheet.
- Roast at 200°C for 10 minutes or until golden brown.
- Remove to cool and add a further tbsp of Peri-Peri Sauce.
- Toss to coat well.
- Serve warm or cold.
- These freeze well and can be kept in an airtight box for up to a week.

with thanks!
The Cluck-ups

We hope you have as much fun with these recipes as we did, it didn't always go to plan as you can see but the end result was always worth it....!

We would love to hear what you thought of our book and any other recipes we could use in the future! You can e-mail us at recipes@nandos.co.uk.

A big Nando's thank you to everyone who helped put this book together, especially the people who had the arduous task of tasting every recipe (you Peri-Peri lucky people) and those who opened their homes and gardens to us and our photographer to help show what fun you can have with Nando's.

Bom Provieto!

❀Nando's❀

OUTDOOR

At last! The collection of
Nando's recipes you've been
asking us for......

Peri-delicious and peri-simple
to make, there's one for every
occasion.

All our favourite outdoor
recipes are at the front of the
book, simply turn the book over
to find our wonderful indoor
recipes.

Enjoy!

Everyone loves a BBQ! Planned or
last minute, it always smells
and tastes the same –
delicious. Always invite the
neighbours, it saves them
drooling over the fence…

The Perfect Barbecue

A picnic is the ultimate getaway,
nothing to do but enjoy the food
and the company and .....relax!
The food should be easy-going
and delicious, chilled soup and
a throw-together salad fit
the bill perfectly...

famous

The man's kitchen!

Moving to the UK after many years in South Africa, the obvious house warming party for Karin & Ian was a BBQ, to show their new neighbours how to do it properly! In the warmth of South Africa, outdoor cooking is very popular and the braai is at the heart of many mealtimes. Karin now works for the Nando's Grocery team in the north of England and is in charge of keeping the mood light and sunny whenever it rains!

"When we braai I can get the meat marinating and salads made in advance, then sit with a glass of wine watching Ian do the cooking for a change – my favourite kind of meal. The kids always enjoy it too because it means we eat outside and they can play on the grass while we finish the wine."

Ian's braai tips:

- Firstly, build a shelter over the braai – it rains more often than not in the U.K!
- Don't put on too much coal to begin with and remember to leave a space between the coals and the grill.
- Don't cook on the braai until you can hold your hand 6 inches over the coals for a few seconds. The coals should be white at this stage.
- Poultry is cooked when the juices run clear.
- Keep on basting regularly during cooking.
- Leave meat to rest for several minutes after cooking.

Nando's Portuguese BBQ Burger with Tomato & Coriander Salsa

Ingredients

400g	lean beef mince
50g	finely diced onion
2g	salt
75ml	Nando's Portuguese BBQ Marinade
2	beaten eggs (to bind)
4	Portuguese bread rolls
	flour (to bind)

Salsa Ingredients

1	finely chopped tomato (150g)
50g	finely diced onion
5g	finely chopped coriander leaf
2g	salt
3 tsp	Nando's Hot Peri Peri Sauce

Method:

- Mix mince, chopped onion, salt, eggs and marinade together then form 4 equal sized patties (dust with flour to bind).
- Place patties on grill (or BBQ) and cook for 8 - 10 minutes.
- Mix together the salsa ingredients (or use a blender if you prefer).

Serve burgers on freshly buttered rolls with generous helpings of Salsa.

I can't tell you how nice these burgers are, you just have to try them!

Chicken Satays with Sun-dried Tomatoes

Ingredients

1kg	filleted chicken breasts
1 jar	Nando's Sun-dried Tomato & Basil Marinade (or Hot Peri-Peri Marinade)
2 tbsp	honey (warmed)
200g	sun-dried tomatoes
	fresh basil leaves chopped

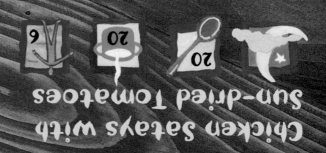

Method:

• Cut each chicken breast into thin strips and weave onto small skewers with the sun-dried tomatoes.

• Mix the marinade, honey and basil leaves, pour over the chicken skewers and allow to marinate for several hours, preferably overnight (covered, in the fridge).

• Cook on a medium hot, lightly greased barbecue or flat plate for 5 – 6 minutes on either side turning often until thoroughly cooked.

Serve with a simple dip of plain yoghurt, chopped cucumber, a pinch of cumin and a teaspoon of Nando's Peri-Peri.

Nando's Drumsticks

Your imagination is the only limit when it comes to inspired drumsticks! To ensure they're cooked through give them a few minutes in the microwave or 20 mins in the oven before barbecuing.

Spicy Drumsticks

Ingredients

8	chicken drumsticks
1 jar	Nando's Sun-dried Tomato & Basil Marinade
4 tbsp	flour
2 tsp	salt
1 tsp	fresh ground black pepper
1/2 tsp	cayenne pepper
1 tsp	paprika

Method:

- Marinate the drumsticks.
- Put the flour and spices in a plastic bag and mix thoroughly.
- Add the drumsticks and shake until well coated.
- Place the pieces on a baking rack and allow to dry for 30 minutes.
- Heat the oil to 180°C and fry the chicken for 12-16 minutes until golden brown all over.
- Serve with a fresh tomato, basil and sweet chilli salsa.

Sweet & Sticky Drumsticks

Ingredients

8	chicken drumsticks
1 jar	Nando's Sweet Peri-Peri Sauce

Method:

- Marinate the drumsticks for about 25 minutes
- BBQ over a low heat, turning and basting frequently

Simple Drumsticks

Ingredients

8	chicken drumsticks
1 jar	Nando's Marinade (use your favourite flavour!)

Method:

- Marinate the drumsticks.
- Grill over hot coals until cooked.

Sun-dried Tomato & Chicken Pasta Salad

Ingredients

500g	chicken fillets sliced and marinated in
1 jar	Nando's Sun-dried Tomato & Basil Marinade
300g	fusilli pasta
3 tbsp	olive oil
2 cloves	crushed garlic
1	medium onion cut into slivers
1	green pepper/capsicum cut into slivers
1	red pepper/capsicum cut into slivers
5 tbsp	black olives, pitted and chopped
3 tbsp	capers
4 tbsp	coarsely chopped fresh parsley

Method:

- Cook pasta according to manufacturer's instruction and drain.
- In a deep sided frying pan, heat up the olive oil and sauté the garlic and onion until glossy/translucent.
- Add the pepper/capsicum strips and sauté for 2 minutes then set aside.
- Cook the chicken in the marinade for 5-7 mins (until brown).
- Add the garlic, onion and pepper/capsicum strips along with the capers and black olives.
- Cook for another 2-3 minutes, until the chicken is thoroughly cooked.
- Add cooked pasta and stir through to mix evenly.
- Add the fresh parsley and stir through just before serving.

Fish with Mango and Radish Salsa

Ingredients

4	fish fillets e.g. plaice
1 jar	Nando's Lemon & Rosemary Marinade
2 tbsp	plain flour
3 tbsp	fresh coriander, chopped
2 tbsp	butter
	sea salt and freshly ground pepper

Salsa Ingredients

8	radishes, chopped
1	ripe mango, diced
2 tsp	mustard seeds
2 tsp	mint, finely chopped
3 tbsp	Nando's Medium Peri Peri Sauce
	juice of 1 fresh lime
2 tsp	olive oil
	coriander, chopped

Method:

- Marinate fish in marinade.
- Mix salsa ingredients together and set aside.
- Preheat grill to medium.
- Season the flour with the salt and pepper and mix in the chopped coriander.
- Dip flesh side of each fish fillet into the mixture to coat evenly and lay skin side down on the grill rack.
- Top each fish fillet with a knob of butter and grill for 5 – 7 minutes or until cooked.
- To serve top with salsa.

If Barbecuing use monkfish instead of plaice as it will hold together better.

Roasted Reds Lentil and Rice Risotto

Ingredients

1	onion, chopped
4 tbsp	olive oil
400g	long grain rice
100g	brown lentils, soaked
1 jar	Nando's Roasted Reds Cooking Sauce
400ml	stock
2	bay leaves
1/2 tsp	salt
	fresh coriander to serve

Method:

- Preheat the oven to 180°C.
- Heat the olive oil in a pot with a lid and sweat the onions and rice.
- Add the stock and cooking sauce and bring to boiling point.
- Add lentils and bay leaves and stir.
- Cover and place in the oven for 20 minutes
- Fluff with a fork to separate.
- Season to taste with salt and scatter with fresh coriander.

BBQ Chilli Corn

Ingredients

6	corn cobs with husks	
60g	melted butter	
4 tbsp	Nando's Hot or Medium Peri-Peri Sauce	

Method:

Remove most of the husks from the corn. Use remaining husk to wrap around corn as a handle. Combine butter and Peri-Peri and brush over corn. Barbecue over hot coals until tender, basting often.

14

Perfect-for-the-BBQ Stuffed Tomatoes

Ingredients

300g	cooked white rice	
4 tbsp	Nando's Lime & Coriander Marinade	
12	ripe tomatoes	
2 tbsp	chopped chives	
2 tbsp	torn basil	
2 tbsp	finely chopped parsley	
1 tbsp	small capers	
1	red pepper/capsicum, diced small	
1	yellow pepper, diced small	

Method:

• Slice the top off each tomato and keep aside. Scoop out the juice and seeds into a bowl and retain.
• Season the inside of each tomato and turn upside down on paper towels to drain.
• Chop the scooped-out tomato flesh and tomato lids and mix these with the cooked rice and remaining ingredients.
• Pile the rice into the tomatoes and serve with salad.

Simple Potato Wedges

Ingredients

2 or 3	large baking potatoes
4 tbsp	Nando's Sun-dried Tomato Marinade or Hot Peri-Peri Marinade
1 tbsp	olive oil
2 tbsp	sun-dried tomatoes
1 tbsp	black olives, pitted & sliced
	good handful fresh basil, torn

Method:

- Peel and cut each potato into wedges (or if you prefer into small dice).
- Parboil the wedges for 10 minutes (if you're using dice 5 minutes will be plenty).
- Meanwhile mix all the remaining ingredients together in a large bowl.
- Drain the potatoes and allow to sit and steam to evaporate any moisture.
- Tip the potatoes into the bowl and stir gently. Allow to marinate for up to an hour.
- Roast the potatoes in a tin lined with non-stick paper at 200°C for 40 minutes, turning every 15 minutes to give a good even colour.

Serve with fresh basil.

Peri-Easy picnics

With beautiful weather all-year-round in South Africa it's an easy task for Lee-Ann to organise an after-work picnic for her Nando's family – but only if they promise not to talk about work!

"Enjoying some time with my friends really chills me out and I just love to be outside after a long day at the office, with fresh air and space all around me, and best of all, no phones. It's a lovely feeling to pack up some simple food and a bottle of wine and get away from it all, even if it's just to the local park. Taking a few beers and some outdoor games keeps the lads busy whilst we unpack the food and enjoy a gossip!"

Lee-Ann
x

Spicy Gazpacho Soup

Ingredients

1kg	firm & ripe tomatoes (this determines the quality of the flavour)
1	green pepper/capsicum, cut into 5mm cubes
1/2	cucumber, diced into 5mm cubes
1	medium onion, diced into 5mm cubes
1 clove	freshly crushed garlic
2 tsp	salt
4 tbsp	olive oil
2 tbsp	balsamic vinegar (or white wine vinegar for a clearer colour)
6	ice cubes crushed
3	basil leaves, finely chopped
3 tsp	Nando's Medium (or Hot) Peri-Peri Sauce black pepper to taste, 1 day old Foccacia roll

Method:

- Cut the tomatoes in half, and grate with a coarse grater, by pressing the cut side against the grater.
- Blend the tomato pulp with the pepper/capsicum, cucumber, onion, and garlic then place in the fridge to cool.
- In the meantime, blend the salt, olive oil, vinegar, basil and Peri-Peri and pour over the tomato mixture.
- Cut the Foccacia into 1 inch cubes.
- Just before serving, stir in the Foccacia chunks, the crushed ice, and season with crushed black pepper. Salt may be adjusted now.

The secret is to serve this soup as cold as possible to appreciate the delicate taste.

Peri-Peri Picnic Bread

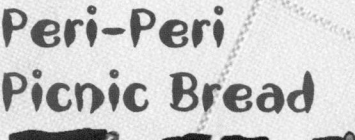

20   10   4

Ingredients

1	**large farmstyle round bread**
1	**small aubergine/brinjal**
1	**large yellow pepper/capsicum**
1	**large red pepper/capsicum**
3 tbsp	**olive oil**
3 cloves	**crushed garlic**
500g	**rump minute steaks (or 500g beef chunk sliced into very thin slices)**
1 jar	**Nando's Hot Peri-Peri or Roasted Red Marinade**

Method:

- Marinate the beef in the marinade for a couple of hours.

- Cut off the top of the bread (to form a lid) and hollow out the inside of the loaf, leaving just a narrow layer of bread all round.

- Slice the aubergine/brinjal into thin slices, and layer on a flat baking sheet.

- De-seed the peppers/capsicum and cut into segments. Place next to the aubergine on the baking sheet.

- Drizzle with the olive oil and garlic and grill until slightly charred. Remove from heat.

- Pan-fry the beef quickly (1 minute on each side to taste), set aside to rest.

- Fill the bread alternating layers of peppers, aubergine and beef.

- Pour the pan juices over the layers.

- Press all the layers down firmly and replace the lid of the bread.

- Slice into chunks and serve with a green salad.

Best left for a while to let the flavours develop. Serve hot or cold.

Tortilla Wraps with Chicken & Salsa

Perfect for a summer lunch outside, and the Salsa is so addictive you'll find yourself making it to go with almost everything.

Ingredients

- 4 **chicken breast fillets**
- 1 jar **Nando's Sun-dried Tomato & Basil Marinade**
- 8 **tortilla wraps**
- 1 **sliced avocado**
- 1 **yellow pepper/capsicum**
- 1 **tub sour cream**

Salsa Ingredients

- 2 **pitted nectarines, finely chopped**
- 1 tsp **freshly grated ginger**
- 2 tsp **finely chopped coriander leaf**
- 1/2 tsp **sea salt**
- 4 tsp **Nando's Hot Sweet Peri-Peri Sauce**

Try using different flavoured tortilla wraps

Method:

- Preheat the grill to medium.
- In the meantime wrap each chicken breast in cling film and evenly flatten using a meat tenderiser (or rolling pin!) then remove clingfilm and place chicken in a bowl with the marinade.
- Allow to marinate for at least 15 minutes.
- Core and deseed the yellow pepper/capsicum and grill with the chicken fillets for 8 -10 minutes until charred in appearance.
- Mix the salsa ingredients together.
- Preheat tortilla wraps for 8 seconds in the microwave.
- Lightly dress half the tortilla wraps with sour cream to taste.
- Slice the chicken fillets and pepper/capsicum lengthways into strips.
- Fill the wrap with the sliced avocado, chicken and pepper/capsicum.
- Finish off with a generous helping of the nectarine salsa.

Lemon Chicken Salad

Ingredients

1/2 jar	Nando's Fresh Lemon Cooking Sauce
4 tbsp	greek or low fat yoghurt
4 tbsp	mayonnaise
350g	leftover cooked cold chicken, pulled into chunks
3	celery sticks, sliced
4	tomatoes, quartered
	selection of salad leaves
1	handful pumpkin and sunflower seeds
	chopped herbs to garnish; chives or parsley

Method:

· Mix the cooking sauce with the yoghurt and mayonnaise.

· Add the chicken and celery.

· Fill a salad bowl or individual plates with a selection of leaves and the tomato quarters.

· Top with the lemon chicken mixture and garnish with nuts and seeds, chopped herbs and a few twists of freshly ground black pepper.

Panzanella

 35   40  4

+1 hour standing time

Ingredients

1 small	**Ciabatta loaf (stale)**
1/2	**cucumber, cut into chunks**
1	**large sweet Spanish onion, roughly cut**
4	**ripe tomatoes**
4 tbsp	**Nando's Hot Peri-Peri Marinade**
1	**clove garlic, crushed**
1	**handful fresh basil**

1	**red pepper/capsicum**
1	**yellow pepper/capsicum**
4	**anchovy fillets, finely chopped**
1 tbsp	**capers**
	olive oil
	sea salt & cracked black pepper

Method:

- Preheat the oven to 200°C.

- Roast the peppers/capsicums in a little olive oil, salt and pepper for 30-40 minutes. When cool, peel and cut into chunks.

- Put the cucumber and onions in a colander, lightly salt them and allow to drain for 20 minutes.

- Halve the tomatoes and scoop the juice and inner flesh into a large bowl, chop or squash this with your hands and set aside. Chop the empty tomato halves and add to the bowl.

- Add all the remaining ingredients along with the cucumber, onion and pepper/capsicum. Tear the Ciabatta and then layer with the tomato mixture in serving dishes.

- Allow to stand for an hour at room temperature for the flavours to develop then serve with an excellent olive oil on the side for drizzling.

Aubergine Puree & Medium Peri-Peri Dip

- 250g aubergine puree
- 30g Nando's Medium Peri-Peri Sauce

Mix together and serve as a dip with vegetables or roast lamb.

Smoked Trout Dip

- 200g smoked trout fillets
- 150g Greek yoghurt
- 1/2 jar Nando's Lemon & Rosemary Marinade
- 1 lemon, juice and zest
- 1 small bunch parsley, chopped

Blend the trout in a food processor, add the remaining ingredients and serve with toasted pitta bread.

Coriander Yoghurt Dip

- 250g Greek yoghurt or low fat yoghurt
- 1 bunch coriander, chopped
- 1 lime, juice and zest
- 1 tbsp Nando's Medium or Hot Peri-Peri Sauce

Mix all the ingredients together and serve.

Peri-Peri Humous

Stir 2 tbsp of Nando's Hot Peri-Peri Sauce into a tub of humous.

Simply serve as a dip with breadsticks or make a meal of it by serving in a jacket potato or with roast lamb.

Peri-Peri Guacamole

- 1 tub guacamole
- 1 tsp Nando's Hot Peri-Peri Sauce
- 1/2 red pepper/capsicum, diced chopped coriander
- 1/2 avocado, diced

Mix everything together and serve with tortilla chips, or in a baked potato.

Sweet Peri-Peri Cream Cheese

Stir 2 tbsp of Nando's Sweet Peri-Peri Sauce into a tub of cream cheese and serve on toast or in a jacket potato.

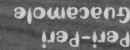

Portuguese BBQ Butter

- 125g butter, softened
- 40g Nando's Portuguese BBQ Marinade
- 20g dried apricots, chopped finely
- 5g parsley, chopped

- In a bowl mix together the marinade and butter.
- Stir in the apricots and parsley.
- Spoon onto a sheet of greaseproof paper or aluminium foil and roll it into a sausage shape.
- Chill well before slicing.

※ Brilliant for freezing.

Nectarine Salsa

- 4 pitted nectarines, chopped
- 1 tsp freshly grated ginger
- 2 tbsp finely chopped coriander leaf
- 1/2 tsp salt
- 3 tsp Nando's Hot Sweet Peri-Peri Sauce

Mix all the ingredients together and serve.

Hot Peri-Peri Butter

- 125g butter, softened
- 40g Nando's Hot Peri-Peri Sauce
- 15g red pepper, chopped finely
- 5g parsley, chopped

- In a bowl mix together the hot peri-peri and butter.
- Stir in the red pepper and parsley.
- Spoon onto a sheet of greaseproof paper or aluminium foil and roll it into a sausage shape.
- Chill well before slicing.

※ Brilliant for freezing.

Créme Fraiche & Portuguese BBQ Dip

- 250g créme fraiche
- 60g Nando's Portuguese BBQ marinade

Mix together and serve as a dip with vegetables or as a sauce to accompany chicken, fish kebabs or jacket potatoes.

Fruit Salsa

- 1 small red chilli, deseeded and sliced finely
- 8 cherry tomatoes cut in quarters
- 1/2 bunch spring onions, sliced finely
- 1/2 papaya, de-pipped and diced
- 1/2 lime, juiced and zested
- 1/2 mango, peeled and diced
- 2 tsp Nando's Garlic Peri-Peri Sauce
  salt and pepper
- 1 tbsp olive oil

Mix all the ingredients together and serve.